TOP SECRET SCIENCE IN
THE MILITARY

James Bow

CRABTREE
PUBLISHING COMPANY
WWW.CRABTREEBOOKS.COM

TOP SECRET SCIENCE

Author: James Bow

Editors: Sarah Eason, Honor Head, Claudia Martin, and Ellen Rodger

Proofreaders: Sally Scrivener, Tracey Kelly, and Wendy Scavuzzo

Editorial director: Kathy Middleton

Design: Jeni Child and Paul Myerscough

Cover design: Paul Myerscough and Jeni Child

Photo research: Rachel Blount

Production coordinator and prepress technician: Ken Wright

Print coordinator: Katherine Berti

Consultant: David Hawksett

Produced for Crabtree Publishing by Calcium Creative

Photo Credits:

t=Top, tr=Top Right, tl=Top Left

Inside: Department of Defense: p. 36; Shutterstock: Andrey Popov: pp. 3, 37; Andrey Armyagov: pp. 32–33t; Best-Backgrounds: p. 16; Boscorelli: p. 7r; Chesky: p. 43b; Cybrain: pp. 40–41b;Andy Dean Photography: pp. 28–29t; Dr Manager: p. 14t; Everett Historical: p. 8; Icsnaps: p. 31; Microgen: p. 45b; Gianluca D.Muscelli: pp. 1, 41r; PressLab: p. 10; Science photo: p. 39r; Sue Stokes: p. 13; WindVector: pp. 6–7t, 45t; U. S. Air Force: p. 19; U.S. Air Force photo/Staff Sgt. Aaron D. Allmon II: p. 9; Airman 1st Class Christopher Griffin: p. 22c; Master Sgt. Lek Mateo: pp. 22–23b; U. S. Army: U.S. Army photo by Devin Fisher: p. 30; University of Rochester: J. Adam Fenster: p. 21; Wikimedia Commons: p. 18; Fred W. Baker III: p. 12; Benjamint444: p. 43r; Y. Colombe/NIST: pp. 38–39; Daderot: p. 24t; DARPA: p. 42; Sgt. Sarah Enos: pp. 4–5t; Benjamin D. Esham (bdesham): p. 11t; Freak of Jesus: p. 35b; Nate Grigg: p. 17; Sgt. 1st Class Michael Guillory: p. 34b; T. Sgt Michael Haggerty, USAF: p. 32; Horton (Capt) War Office Official Photographer: p. 15; Vitaly V. Kuzmin: p. 26b; Republic of Korea Armed Forces: p. 20; Jim Sanborn: p. 11b; Senior Airman Julianne Showalter, U. S. Air Force: p. 27; Antoine Taveneaux: p. 14b; USAF: pp. 24b, 26t; U.S. Army Corps of Engineers, Cold Regions Research and Engineering Laboratory: p. 5b; U. S. Marine Corps photo by Chief Warrant Officer 2 Keith A. Stevenson: pp. 34–35t; U.S. Navy photo courtesy of General Dynamics/Released: p. 25; Tucker M. Yates: p. 29b.

Cover: Shutterstock: Breakermaximus.

Library and Archives Canada Cataloguing in Publication

Bow, James, author
    Top secret science in the military / James Bow.

(Top secret science)
Includes index.
Issued in print and electronic formats.
ISBN 978-0-7787-5995-9 (hardcover).--
ISBN 978-0-7787-6033-7 (softcover).--
ISBN 978-1-4271-2244-5 (HTML)

    1. Military research--Juvenile literature. I. Title.

U390.B69 2019   j355'.07   C2018-905662-2
                                     C2018-905663-0

Library of Congress Cataloging-in-Publication Data

Names: Bow, James, author.
Title: Top secret science in the military / James Bow.
Description: New York, NY : Crabtree Publishing Company, [2019] | Series : Top Secret Science | Includes index.
Identifiers: LCCN 2018053418 (print) | LCCN 2018054436 (ebook) | ISBN 9781427122445 (Electronic) | ISBN 9780778759959 (hardcover : alk. paper) | ISBN 9780778760337 (pbk. : alk. paper)
Subjects: LCSH: Military research--Juvenile literature. | Defense information, Classified--Juvenile literature.
Classification: LCC U390 (ebook) | LCC U390 .B69 2019 (print) | DDC 355/.07--dc23
LC record available at https://lccn.loc.gov/2018053418

Crabtree Publishing Company

www.crabtreebooks.com   1-800-387-7650

Printed in the U.S.A./042019/CG20190215

Published in Canada
Crabtree Publishing
616 Welland Ave.
St. Catharines, ON
L2M 5V6

Published in the United States
Crabtree Publishing
PMB 59051
350 Fifth Avenue, 59th Floor
New York, NY 10118

Published in the United Kingdom
Crabtree Publishing
Maritime House
Basin Road North, Hove
BN41 1WR

Published in Australia
Crabtree Publishing
Unit 3 – 5 Currumbin Court
Capalaba
QLD 4157

CONTENTS

[MATCH]

John Doe

AGE 35   HEIGHT 5'11"

Occupation Manager

Interests Technology, VR, Travel

Location London

ID 34593457834   HASHCODE 2AB4 CF23 EF98 DA57
CHECKSUM 893428657843578265785   DB GeneralPublic2A

MATCH 99%

CHAPTER 1

THE SECRECY WEAPON

On the battlefield, fighting forces look for any means necessary to defeat their enemy, while taking as few losses as possible. On today's battlefields, it is not the bigger or braver army that gets the upper hand—it is the army with the most **technologically** advanced weapons and defenses. To have this advantage, armies go to great lengths to keep their scientific breakthroughs a secret.

SECRET WEAPONS

Ever since gunpowder was first used to fire weapons in tenth-century China, inventing new weapons—and keeping the new inventions secret—has been a key part of military planning. Today, gunpowder is a thing of the past, except in fireworks. Weapons currently in development make use of scientific breakthroughs that are so new, only a few people understand them. These breakthroughs include high-energy beams of **particles** and **sonic** assaults, which use sound to injure or confuse the enemy.

Injury on the battlefield can be avoided by using secrecy and surprise against an enemy force.

SECRETS ON THE BATTLEFIELD

In addition to building weapons, the latest technology can help keep fighting forces informed and protect their secrets. Powerful computers are used to code messages to keep them secret from the enemy. Other tactics used to fool the enemy include **decoys** and camouflage. Militaries are building bigger and better decoys to draw enemy soldiers out into the open, and finding extraordinary ways to camouflage soldiers and equipment. They are also using high-tech science to break enemy **codes**, defeat enemy decoys, and see through camouflage.

DARK SCIENCE SECRETS

In the 1960s, the United States military built a secret base called Camp Century under the ice in Greenland. Officially, Camp Century was a science station, but in reality, it hid a deeper secret. In Project Iceworm, the U.S. military dug tunnels into the ice as part of a plan to store medium-range **ballistic missiles** to use against Russia. It proved too difficult to build such a base, however, and Project Iceworm was abandoned in 1967. The United States thought the ice would keep the project hidden forever, but today the Greenland ice is melting due to **climate change**. This is revealing the base, and the secrets that the U.S. military left behind.

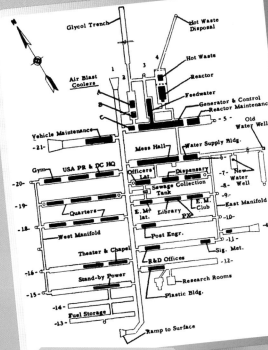

This 1965 top secret plan shows the network of ice tunnels at Camp Century, which were used to hide long-range missiles.

SECRETS AS WEAPONS

Military forces want to keep information secret about where or how troops will strike, so the enemy will not be prepared when the attack happens. But information can be used as a weapon, too. False information can fool enemy soldiers, convincing them that an attack is coming from one place when, in fact, it will come from another. The actual attack is then a surprise and more likely to succeed.

Today, aerial photographs like this one can show detailed images of an enemy's military base.

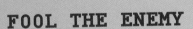

TARGET 1   TARGE

TARGET 2   TARGE

FOOL THE ENEMY

The military uses a number of tricks to fool the enemy. In 1943, during World War II (1939–1945), the **Soviet Union** fought the invading German Army in Kursk, south of Moscow, Russia. The Soviet army knew the Germans were listening to their radio broadcasts, so it sent fake radio reports saying there were not enough troops to defend the city. At the same time, the Soviet army attacked the Germans, then retreated. This convinced the Germans that the Soviets were weak and desperate. Meanwhile, the Soviet army secretly moved in supplies and soldiers during the night, laying minefields, and improving defenses. When the Germans attacked, they discovered the Soviets had nearly 4,000 more tanks and more than 1 million more soldiers than they had expected. The Soviet victory stopped the German advance into Russia and changed the entire course of the war.

VIRTUAL REALITY TACTICS

Virtual reality (VR) is a technology that uses complex computer programs and headsets to give the user the sense that they have entered another world. VR is not just for gaming: militaries have adopted the technology as a training method, to give soldiers the sense of being on the battlefield without putting them in danger. When it comes to planning secret attacks and unexpected counterattacks, VR **simulations** of battlefields are ideal. They help officers learn new methods of using troops in different battlefield scenarios. On the battlefield, this would cost lives. The U.S. army uses the Virtual Squad Training System (VSTS), which allows soldiers to practice tactics as well as to handle the newest weapons and vehicles.

Drone technology has made it more difficult to hide soldiers and military vehicles from the enemy.

TOMORROW'S SECRETS

Technology is making it more difficult for an army to fool the enemy. To get clear pictures of enemy positions, militaries rely on aerial photographs. However, planes are an easy target for the enemy on the ground. As a result, the military has turned to **unmanned aerial vehicles (UAVs)**. UAV technology has advanced so much that unmanned drones are now used to take aerial photographs of the enemy. Drones are small and therefore difficult to detect. They also have **sensors** that can pick up things that are invisible to the human eye, such as the body heat of hiding soldiers.

SUPERWEAPONS

Military scientists are always looking for ways to make bigger and better weapons. Between 1942 and 1946, the United States, United Kingdom, and Canada secretly worked together to build an **atomic bomb** to use against the enemy during World War II. This devastating bomb was dropped on the Japanese cities of Hiroshima and Nagasaki in 1945, killing 129,000–226,000 people. Today's secret weapons have the power to be just as deadly—and even more accurate.

The Manhattan Project created one of the most deadly weapons ever-the atomic bomb.

THE VANISHED CITY

The code name for the project to build an atomic bomb was "the Manhattan Project." To keep the research secret, the U.S. government made a city disappear! In 1942, the government bought the homes of Oak Ridge, Tennessee, and ordered the 1,000 residents to leave. Oak Ridge was then removed from official government maps. Security officials searched everyone who left the site. Thanks to these efforts, only a few dozen Americans knew the details of the atomic bombs before they were dropped on Japan. The destruction caused by the bombs shocked even the scientists who made them. Governments soon realized that atomic bombs and other **nuclear weapons** threatened all life on Earth. From 1968, the United States and 189 other countries signed the Nuclear Non-Proliferation Treaty, promising not to share technology that could help new countries build nuclear weapons. Despite this, many people worry that countries such as North Korea are working to build nuclear weapons in secret.

NEW TECHNOLOGY

The atomic bombs used against Japan got their destructive force from nuclear reactions, by splitting apart the **nuclei** of **atoms**. Atoms are tiny particles that are the building blocks for everything on Earth. Splitting them releases a massive amount of energy. Today, some weapons in development make use of newer breakthroughs in our understanding of atoms and the tiny particles (called **subatomic particles**) inside them. Particle-beam weapons would use a high-energy beam of subatomic particles to damage the atoms in their target. This would kill a human being. The U.S. military is researching such weapons to be used against incoming enemy missiles. It is vital that the research remains a secret so these weapons can never be used against people.

Stealth planes have made it possible for the military to spy on and track enemies from the air, completely undetected.

DARK SCIENCE SECRETS

The U.S. Air Force has experimented with stealth technology since the 1950s. It has successfully created stealth planes, which are less visible to the human eye because of the way light bounces off them. The planes reflect their surroundings. Stealth planes are also designed so that they are less likely to be picked up and tracked by **radar**. This allows them to make raids or to take spy photos over countries without being caught. While stealth planes are not a secret, the military keeps their abilities and their technology carefully guarded and top secret.

CHAPTER 2

CODES AND CODE BREAKERS

Codes are a way for the military to send information in a form that only the people intended to read it can understand. Information can be kept secret by replacing words and letters with symbols, signs, numbers, or random strings of letters. In the past, this was done with books of code or simple machines. Today, powerful computers use mathematical rules called algorithms to code and decode military messages.

ENCRYPTION

Encryption is a way of encoding a message so it can only be read by its chosen recipient. Encryption uses a **cipher**, a set of well-defined steps for encoding the information. For example, the ROT-13 cipher changes each letter to one that is 13 letters farther along in the alphabet. The problem with such simple ciphers is that, with enough attempts, anyone can figure them out.

Military information can win or lose a war. Soldiers communicate using code to keep their movements top secret.

The ROT-13 cipher is simple to decode. AES-256 encryption has at least 256 times more possibilities for every letter.

AES-256

"Military-grade" encryption is the level of encryption used by militaries, governments, and unfortunately, some terrorist groups to keep their computer messages secret. One form of military-grade encryption is known as AES-256. AES stands for Advanced Encryption Standard. The computer algorithm divides the data (or information) into small chunks, then scrambles them beyond recognition a total of 14 times. On top

of this, it sprinkles random nonsense data—called "salt"—over the encrypted material, then scrambles it all over again. The data can only be decrypted by someone with the correct password. The password starts the reverse process, removing the salt and unscrambling the data.

DARK SCIENCE SECRETS

In 1988, the U.S. Central **Intelligence Agency** (CIA) ordered a 12-foot-tall (3.6-m) sculpture to be built outside their headquarters in Washington, D.C. Called Kryptos, it contains four coded messages that the CIA challenged other intelligence agencies to decode. A team from the **National Security** Agency (NSA) took up the challenge and solved three of the four messages by 1993. The fourth code remains unsolved.

Kryptos is proof that some codes are too difficult to break! To date, only the CIA has the answer.

TIME TO TRANSLATE

Language is itself a code, with the sounds we make and the letters we write representing our thoughts. When people who speak different languages meet, they need to crack the other's code, by learning the new language, hiring a human translator—or using extraordinary new computer programs to do all the work for them.

Communicating with local people is vital so that the military can learn about possible threats.

COMBAT COMMUNICATION

Speaking in a language that the people around you cannot understand is an effective way of keeping secrets. However, when soldiers are working in another country, they need to be able to crack the code of the local language, so that they can protect themselves from attack—and also help people.

The U.S. military is currently trying out new computer systems that translate languages as they are spoken. The Machine Foreign Language Translation System (MFLTS) allows U.S. soldiers and local people in other countries to speak to each other. At present, this system is only programmed to translate spoken Pashto, a language spoken in Afghanistan, and Iraqi Arabic, plus written Arabic. These are languages that the U.S. military comes across daily during its work in these countries. War and terrorism have made Afghanistan and Iraq unstable. U.S. soldiers use MFLTS to speak with locals to protect innocent people, while quickly identifying fighters who pose a threat. In the future, many language packs, suitable for different regions, will be available.

LANGUAGE DEVICES

MFLTS devices are armed with cameras, which means they can capture images of written language. The program is then able to recognize the letters in the images, using optical character recognition (OCR) technology, before translating the words that they form. The devices also have microphones and voice recognition **software**. When we speak, our words have patterns of loud and soft sounds. For example, a hard consonant, like a "t," is a sudden, loud sound. Voice recognition software compares the patterns of loud and soft with the **phonemes**, or speech sounds, in its **database**, then recognizes the whole words that they form. In addition, the MFLTS is programmed to supply useful phrases with one click, both friendly greetings and urgent, life-saving orders.

DARK SCIENCE SECRETS

During World War II, the U.S. military turned to the Navajo Nation, as well as other Native American peoples, to protect its secrets. At the time, the Navajo did not have a written language, and their spoken language was very different from any other language. Non-native speakers had difficulty telling certain tones and phrases apart. This made the language a perfect tool for sending top secret information over the radio. Navajo-speakers were recruited by the Marine Corps, which set up a "Code Talker" school.

This monument to the vital work of the Navajo Code Talkers of World War II stands in Phoenix, Arizona.

CRACKING CODES

Decryption—or code-breaking—allows military commands to figure out what the enemy is secretly planning. Today, decryption is the work of **supercomputers**. Able to perform trillions of calculations per second, supercomputers can test multiple ciphers or combinations of ciphers within minutes. Some of the world's most powerful supercomputers belong to national militaries, including the United States, United Kingdom, and Russia. Eventually, even if a code has military-level encryption, these computers will crack it...

Supercomputers, or hundreds of linked computers working together, run through trillions of possible ciphers.

TURING´S BOMBE

In World War II, the Germans built a complicated device called the Enigma machine, to make coded messages. Enigma could make trillions of different codes. The British military brought in a team of experts, including mathematician Alan Turing, to build a calculating machine that could break the Enigma codes quickly. One of the first machines Turing helped design was called the Bombe. The Bornbe could quickly tell when a possible code combination was wrong, and move on to the next possibility. By the summer of 1941, the Bombe helped drastically cut down the number of British ships being attacked by German submarines, because they had cracked the German codes.

Turing´s code-breaking machines changed the world. They eventually led to the creation of modern-day computers.

DARK SCIENCE SECRETS

During World War II, the British government received intelligence from its Enigma code breakers that the city of Coventry, in England, was going to be bombed by the German air force on November 14, 1940. The government did nothing, so that the Germans would not know that Britain had broken its codes. Over 500 people died, 2,300 homes were destroyed, and the city's great cathedral collapsed.

Today, people still argue over whether the British government should have let the city be destroyed. Many experts suggest that warning Coventry would have let the Germans know the British had cracked Enigma. Long-term, that may have cost even more lives.

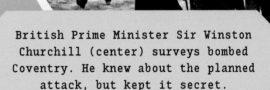

British Prime Minister Sir Winston Churchill (center) surveys bombed Coventry. He knew about the planned attack, but kept it secret.

STEGANOGRAPHY

Since supercomputers can decrypt almost any coded message, some organizations use **steganography** to pretend they are not sending messages at all. Steganography is a way of concealing a computer file, message, image, or video, inside another computer file. One method might be to send a message in a **digital** photograph. Digital photographs are made up of thousands of tiny dots called pixels. The steganographer might change the color of every hundredth pixel to spell out words.

In 2010, the Federal Bureau of Investigation (FBI) accused the Russian intelligence service of using steganography to send messages to its spies. Today, military commands have operatives specially trained in spotting such hidden messages.

HIRED TO HACK

Just as computers have provided better ways to create codes, people called hackers try to crack these codes to break into computer systems. Encryption is difficult to break, but not impossible. Software errors sometimes give hackers a way into computer systems. For this reason, security companies and the military often hire hackers to attack their own networks—to look for weak spots before enemy hackers can find them.

BATTLES ON THE NET

One of the first hacking attacks against the U.S. military took place in the 1980s. A German named Markus Hess stole **classified** information, including space technology files. More recently, in 2008, an unidentified foreign intelligence agency left a USB **flash drive** in a parking lot outside a U.S. Department of Defense building.

A worker picked the USB up and plugged it into their machine. This released a program that infected computers and gave the spies access to classified files. In 2015, the federal government had the personal details of more than 21 million employees hacked and stolen. If used by a foreign power, this information could put national security at risk.

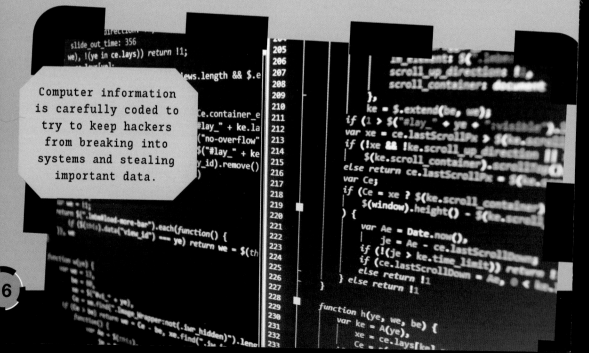

Computer information is carefully coded to try to keep hackers from breaking into systems and stealing important data.

TOP SECRET DEPARTMENT

To respond to attacks, the U.S. military created the Joint Functional Component Command for Network Warfare. While the full nature of this department is top secret, it is known to be a team of hackers whose job it is to defend the U.S. Department of Defense's computer networks from hacker attacks. The department is racing to stay ahead of the hackers working for enemy armies, because wars are increasingly fought online.

Gifted hackers are recruited by the world's top intelligence agencies to protect their systems.

COMPUTER BRAINS

In 2018, scientists at the U.S. Army Research Laboratory suggested that the best way to prevent hackers from stealing information might be to change the way computers are wired. If computers work in a way similar to the human brain, with connections running in many different directions at once and information stored in countless places, it will be far more difficult for hackers to find their secrets.

14:30 PM

TOMORROW'S SECRETS

As hackers break our best encryption codes, scientists are looking at other ways to encrypt data. One solution may lie in our bodies. Scientists at Lancaster University, in the United Kingdom, are monitoring how our hearts and lungs communicate with each other. The two organs send signals to each other constantly, working together to keep us alive. Using the same technique, two computers could send and receive many different encrypted signals, sharing a constantly changing encryption code. Both computers would have to decode the messages together.

DIGITAL WAR

In many countries, computers now run important services such as water, electricity, and the banks. Military experts are warning that these systems could be targets for attack by terrorists or other enemies. This could cause chaos. A deliberate attack against the electrical system could shut down electricity supplies for months, causing loss of power to hospitals, factories, cell phone towers, transportation, and water treatment systems. A deliberate attack against a country's power and computer systems is a deadly threat today, and it is known as cyberwarfare.

MALICIOUS SOFTWARE

Viruses pose a serious threat to world peace today. Many experts predict that the wars of the future will be fought on computers.

Cyberwarfare is fought with computer programs. A computer worm or virus is a program that makes copies of itself so it can spread to other computers. This can be done through e-mails or when victims visit infected websites. A computer virus can rewrite programs on infected computers, lock out users, and take over e-mail programs to send out more copies of itself. These programs can do a huge amount of damage, and even threaten national security.

Some viruses install **ransomware**, which is a system designed to take over and shut down computers. The virus then forces users to pay money to get the use of their computer back. Many experts believe that the Russian military was responsible for the 2017 "NotPetya" ransomware attack against Ukrainian banks, transportation systems, electricity providers, and government offices. Although the spread of the NotPetya virus was halted within a day, it took weeks for all the systems to be fixed.

PRESS ANY KEY!

SLAMMER ATTACK

Some viruses take over thousands of computers and use them to bombard computer systems and websites with fake information. In 2003, the SQL Slammer virus infected half of the U.S. computers that send and receive data across the Internet. Bank machines stopped working and the police 911 emergency service crashed. The virus cost an estimated $1 billion.

TOMORROW'S SECRETS

Spyware is a growing threat to safety and privacy. Spyware is a type of software, often hidden inside ordinary software, that secretly installs itself on a computer or cell phone. The spyware can then take the user's personal information, such as their bank details, and monitor their Internet searches, phone calls, and text messages. In 2018, it was discovered that Iranian hackers, possibly linked to the Iranian government, had installed spyware on the cell phones of hundreds of Iranians.

STUXNET ATTACK

In 2010, security experts uncovered the Stuxnet computer worm. One of its features was to target nuclear research stations. The worm ruined one-fifth of the machines that Iran was using to process nuclear material or to build a nuclear bomb. Experts believe the worm was developed by the United States to destroy Iran's nuclear program. It is likely that other similar top secret viruses will be used to attack potential enemies in the future.

Today, the military is constantly on the lookout for potential cyberattacks that could bring down its computer systems.

HIDE AND SEEK

It was not until the early twentieth century that militaries made camouflage a standard part of their uniforms. Before that time, there was so much confusion and smoke on the battlefield that soldiers usually wore bright uniforms to make sure their own side would not shoot them. Modern warfare involves high-tech weapons and is fought over huge areas. Today, armies use top secret new science equipment to hide their soldiers, vehicles, and weapons from the enemy.

Leaf-patterned uniforms, face paint, and netting help soldiers hide from enemy eyes during surveillance missions.

CAMOUFLAGE UNIFORMS

The army uses camouflage to keep enemy **surveillance** planes or scouts from seeing and targeting their soldiers. The type of camouflage used depends on the type of area soldiers are in. For example, camouflage uniforms for U.S. soldiers fighting in the green jungles of Vietnam would be easily seen in the sandy deserts of Iraq. Camouflage is most often used by snipers, who are soldiers with long-range rifles who fire at targets a great distance away. Snipers can spend a long time hiding and waiting for the right moment to fire, so they need to remain camouflaged.

DIGITAL CAMOUFLAGE

Military camouflage is becoming more and more advanced. Scientists are now working on an "invisibility cloak" that will hide soldiers from view. One project is a system of screens and cameras that film the scenery behind an object, such as a soldier or an army vehicle. A screen that shows the scenery is placed in front of the object, thereby hiding it from view. However, technology is also creating ways to overcome camouflage. U.S. soldiers now have **infrared goggles** that detect the heat of bodies hiding in the grass, and microphones that can detect voices and even heartbeats.

This image shows how invisibility cloak technology completely disguises an object, in this case, part of a hand.

TOMORROW'S SECRETS

Infrared sensors used by the military are now so advanced that they can even detect the body heat of soldiers inside a military vehicle. The British defense company BAE Systems has created Adaptiv to fight back against infrared technology. The system covers vehicles in hexagonal panels that can quickly change temperature. The panels **mimic**, or copy, the patterns of heat from plants and other living things around the vehicle. The panels also give off infrared light in such a way that a large military vehicle looks like just an ordinary car when viewed by enemies using infrared sensors. This disguises the vehicle and its soldiers from enemies. Adaptiv also protects military vehicles from weapons such as **heat-seeking missiles**.

SCANNING THE SKY

During the 1930s, the United States and other military powers secretly developed radar systems that could, for the first time, spot approaching enemy planes and boats at a distance. Radar (Radio Detection And Ranging) sends out radio waves and detects when they hit something and bounce back. Radar technology continues to improve. Doppler radar measures the wavelength of radio waves that are bounced back. Radio waves have a shorter wavelength when an object is coming toward a person, and a longer wavelength when it is heading away, revealing in which direction an object is traveling.

Radar has revolutionized the military world. It allows people to see and track objects that could pose a threat.

EARLY WARNINGS

During the 1940s, the United States installed radar stations across the Canadian Arctic and Alaska, called the North Warning System. Its job was to spot missiles from the Soviet Union as they flew over the Arctic Ocean. In 1980, a faulty computer reported that the Soviet Union had launched 2,200 missiles. Thankfully, the report was quickly identified as false.

FALCON

LASER LIGHT

LIght Detection And Ranging (lidar) works in a similar way to radar, but uses light from a **laser**. It sends out pulses of intense light and measures the time taken for the pulses to return. The system is exact enough to build up accurate **three-dimensional (3-D)** maps of land and buildings. Lidar systems on space **satellites** can pick up buildings such as secret army bases carefully hidden beneath thick trees. The military use of lidar remains top secret. However, **North Atlantic Treaty Organization (NATO)** military reports suggest that, along with buildings, lidar can identify hidden targets such as tanks, planes, and other military vehicles.

Lidar is sensitive enough to detect clouds of invisible gas. The use of poisonous gas is banned under international law, but the Syrian government has been accused of using gas against civilians during the Syrian Civil War (2011–). Lidar could prevent future attacks.

Hand-held radar "guns" are useful for detecting the speed of vehicles.

TOMORROW'S SECRETS

The defense company Lockheed Martin is experimenting with an advanced radar system called digital beamforming. Most radar systems simply send out signals and wait for them to bounce back. Digital beamforming systems analyze the signals, and lock onto targets, sending out more beams to track objects as they move. This gives the military a clearer picture of what the radar has found, and far more information about the object.

23

RADAR REACTIONS

Radar has been proven to be extremely effective at finding and targeting incoming planes. The system is so efficient that the military is constantly looking for ways to escape detection by enemy radar systems. Because radar works by picking up radio waves that bounce off objects, military scientists have investigated materials that can absorb the waves and change them into heat, rather than reflecting them back. This keeps radar technology from detecting an object. Military scientists have now developed an exciting technique, called stealth technology, that can hamper enemy radar activity.

Stealth vehicles are covered with materials known as radar-absorbent materials (RAMs).

Stealth planes are designed to be incredibly thin. This design makes them difficult for radar to detect.

DEFEATING RADAR

Iron Ball Paint is a smart material that is used on war planes. It is a liquid full of pyramid-shaped particles. The surfaces of the particles catch radar energy and bounce it around on the surface of the plane, so the energy is not reflected back. Another technique to deal with radar is to make a plane superthin, so it has fewer surfaces that can reflect radar signals.

USING STEALTH

Many military ships now have stealth technology. The ships are designed so that they can move low in the water. This means that less of the ship is exposed, which makes it less of a target for radar. The ships' surfaces also point toward its center and away from the water. This design provides less surface space on which radar signals can bounce.

DARK SCIENCE SECRETS

A vehicle does not need stealth technology if it is so superfast that no missile can catch it. Project Pluto was set up in 1957 to study a nuclear-powered Supersonic Low-Altitude Missile (SLAM). The missile used a nuclear-powered jet engine to accelerate it to speeds of Mach 3, which is three times the speed of sound. By flying close to the ground, the missile avoided radar and could drop nuclear bombs on multiple targets.

Even after dropping its bombs, the U.S. military suggested the missile could continue to fly around for weeks, and destroy more objects. However, the project was canceled in 1964, because it was thought the weapon might encourage the Soviet Union to build a similar missile, which could start a nuclear race. This threat was great enough to outweigh the many advantages of having the missile.

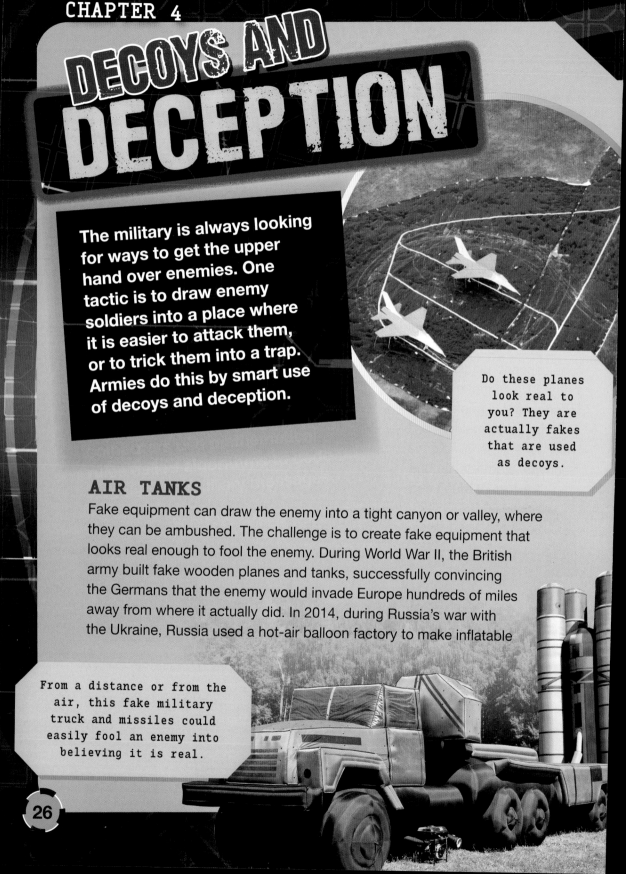

CHAPTER 4

DECOYS AND
DECEPTION

The military is always looking for ways to get the upper hand over enemies. One tactic is to draw enemy soldiers into a place where it is easier to attack them, or to trick them into a trap. Armies do this by smart use of decoys and deception.

Do these planes look real to you? They are actually fakes that are used as decoys.

AIR TANKS

Fake equipment can draw the enemy into a tight canyon or valley, where they can be ambushed. The challenge is to create fake equipment that looks real enough to fool the enemy. During World War II, the British army built fake wooden planes and tanks, successfully convincing the Germans that the enemy would invade Europe hundreds of miles away from where it actually did. In 2014, during Russia's war with the Ukraine, Russia used a hot-air balloon factory to make inflatable

From a distance or from the air, this fake military truck and missiles could easily fool an enemy into believing it is real.

tanks, planes, and missile launchers. These vehicles were so realistic that they tricked soldiers on the ground, even at close quarters. Once enemy soldiers approached, the vehicles were blown up, killing the enemy at the same time.

FOOLING RADAR

Armies also use decoys to fool radar. Military engineers design planes with thin strips of aluminum that release particles called chaff during flight. Chaff can also be released midflight by missiles. The chaff forms a decoy cloud that reflects radar signals. Enemies are fooled into thinking that their radar systems have detected just a cloud, rather than an enemy vehicle.

When military planes are targeted by heat-seeking missiles, one smart decoy technique is to release flares. The heat-seeking missiles then follow the flares rather than the planes.

Chaff is so effective that the U.S. military has been working hard to find ways to tell the difference between enemy targets and chaff clouds. It has developed a new technology called Inverse Synthetic Aperture Radar (ISAR). The technique provides a detailed image of a target behind a chaff cloud. Instead of just a blob on a screen, ISAR clearly shows the wings of a plane or the masts of an enemy ship, as well as the cloud of chaff.

TOMORROW'S SECRETS

Military scientists continue to work on invisibility techniques that can be used to escape radar. In 2018, the Chinese military claimed to have made a "**metamaterial**." When used on planes, the material completely disguises them. This means all planes, not just specially designed stealth planes, could now avoid radar detection. Unfortunately, the details of this metamaterial are unknown because it is a carefully guarded state secret.

SNEAK ATTACKS

Some of the world's militaries and intelligence services use very strange—and cutting-edge—technologies to launch sneak attacks. The victims of such assaults may not even know that they have been attacked. Methods of attack include sonic weapons and "fake news." The results range from physical injury to widespread distress and confusion.

BREAKING NEWS
ONALD TRUMP ELECT
FL
PRESIDE

FAKE NEWS AS A WEAPON

The Russian military is famous for using camouflage, decoys, **propaganda**, and **disinformation** to attack its enemies. This is a form of **psychological warfare** it calls *maskirovka*, and it has helped the Russians win many wars. The Russians have also used the Internet in their *maskirovka* campaigns. Soon after the 2016 U.S. election, officials in the United States investigated how Russia may have helped Donald Trump get elected as president.

Russian hackers broke into the computers of American political parties and released thousands of stolen emails that included damaging

Some people believe that Russian hackers played a role during the 2016 presidential election. The aim of such attacks is to cause instability and confusion.

information about the Democratic Party and its nominee for president, Hillary Clinton. Russian agents secretly joined in with chat rooms and social media. They posted fake news stories to make supporters of each political party hate its opponents. These may not seem like military operations, but such tactics could help one country increase its global power by weakening its enemies.

CHAOS IN CUBA

In 2016 and 2017, employees at the U.S. and Canadian embassies in Cuba complained of hearing loss, headaches, and distress. The Cuban government was accused of using some kind of sonic weapon, or using sound waves, against the workers. Cuba denied they had used any such weapons—and many experts agreed with them. However, sonic weapons are being developed by several militaries. Weapons such as sonic grenades or cannons could make very loud sounds that would destroy the enemy's eardrums, or even kill them. **Ultrasonic** devices would use sound waves outside the human hearing range, which would cause confusion and fear.

DARK SCIENCE SECRETS

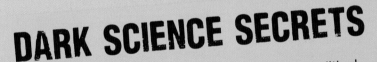

In 2005, the Israeli army was called in to stop a political demonstration that had turned violent, on the border between Israel and Palestine. The army used the "Scream" to break up the riot: a speaker that unleashed noises as loud as 150 decibels (a measure of the strength of sound). That is as loud as a jet plane taking off, and can cause serious ear damage. The piercing noises immediately stopped rioters in their tracks.

The Scream unleashes ear-splitting sounds that are unbearable for the human ear.

MIND GAMES

Armies from countries such as Russia, China, and the United States, have researched the **psychology** of the human mind to discover ways to control human behavior. By doing so, they can force prisoners of war to give up secrets, and even make an enemy give up before the fighting starts.

DRUG DEVELOPMENT

The U.S. and Russian armies have researched a number of drugs to use when questioning prisoners to make them answer questions truthfully. These drugs put prisoners into a trance-like state, similar to hypnosis. In this state, a prisoner is more likely to trust or obey the person talking to them. However, drugging prisoners against their will is widely considered to break the Geneva Conventions, the international rules set down to govern behavior in wartime. In addition, the information given by people while on drugs is unreliable, as they may not know what is truth and what is fiction.

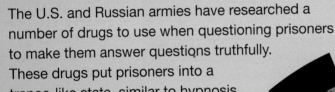

Injuries in wartime may be psychological as well as physical, as shown in this practice drill. Today's militaries could use psychology to harm their enemies as well as help their own soldiers.

EMOTIONAL TRAUMA

The horrors and trauma of war leave mental scars on many veterans. This is called Post-Traumatic Stress Disorder (PTSD). People with PTSD relive traumatic events through nightmares and flashbacks. These are often started by sounds, sights, or smells that remind the sufferer of the situation that caused their trauma, such as loud guns firing on the battlefield. Armies turn to psychology to help their soldiers deal with PTSD. Certain anxiety-reducing drugs may help. Talking to **therapists**, or people who help those suffering from mental health issues, can also help. One way to help people suffering from PTSD might be through VR. Using VR goggles, doctors can recreate the environment in which the original trauma occurred. By returning to the trauma situation in a safe setting, sufferers can begin to overcome problems.

Soldiers can experience PTSD for many years following their involvement in wars.

DARK SCIENCE SECRETS

In the 1950s, the U.S. government experimented with mind control through a program called MKUltra. A Canadian psychologist named Dr. Donald Ewan Cameron tried to remove and reprogram memories and to make his test subjects more obedient. He used powerful drugs on unknowing psychiatric patients in a Montreal hospital, also using constant noise to prevent them from sleeping. The experiments did terrible psychological damage to the patients. The public did not know about the experiments and MKUltra became a major scandal when discovered years later. This led to the Canadian government paying the survivors millions of dollars.

CHAPTER 5

A WORLD WITHOUT SECRETS

A good way to see what your enemy is doing is from the sky. Before satellites, military spying relied on planes to take photographs of the other side's activities, but planes can be shot down. The best place to spy on your enemy is from space. Objects in space are impossible to hit with ordinary weapons, and now spy satellite technology can even show details as small as a car license plate!

The SR-71 Blackbird was a spy plane for viewing enemy territory.

SKY HIGH

Today's satellite systems can help soldiers avoid enemy vehicles and other threats as they travel through unknown landscapes. **Global Positioning System (GPS)** satellites send radio waves to receivers on the ground. By calculating the distance to three or more satellites, a GPS receiver held by a soldier can figure out exactly where it is. This technology is combined with military satellites equipped with cameras and lidar (see page 23), which create extremely accurate pictures of the terrain and its threats.

SATELLITE JAMMERS

The military uses many techniques to avoid satellite detection, including signal jammers. Signal jammers produce a burst of radio signals that swamp satellite signals and keep systems such as GPS receivers from working. Currently, signal jammer devices are based on the ground, but Russia and China are looking at ways to build satellites that jam other satellites from space.

Anti-satellite weapons (ASATs) are designed to destroy enemy satellites. These weapons make use of nuclear explosions, high-energy pulses, or lasers. Although ASATs have never been used in warfare, the U.S. used one to destroy one of its own, broken satellites in 2008.

In the future, new weapons such as high-powered lasers mounted on airplanes could be used to shoot down satellites.

TOMORROW'S SECRETS

There are cameras everywhere in society today, from security cameras in public buildings, to cameras on our phones. Computer worms that can turn these cameras on without our knowledge already exist. While there are no known plans by any army to take over our cameras and listen in to our conversations before an invasion, some people are increasingly worried about their privacy. Some are even putting black tape over their laptop cameras to keep people from spying on them.

DRONE WARFARE

Robots are the future in the world of military surveillance. Rather than a pilot flying a plane on a risky spy mission, a drone does the job instead. Since drones are smaller and lighter than piloted planes, they can often fly faster, turn more quickly, and travel farther before needing to refuel. These characteristics make them excellent devices for carrying out enemy surveillance missions. More controversially, since 2001, drones have been frequently used by the United States to fire missiles at enemy targets.

Not all drones are tiny. The Little Bird H-6U helicopter weighs 2,200 pounds (1,000 kg).

FINDING THE ENEMY

The U.S. military invaded Iraq in 2002 and took over the country. In 2004, however, they were having trouble keeping order. Rebels planted bombs on roads to explode as troops passed by. To deal with this, a surveillance company set up Operation Angel Fire. A plane flying 8,200 feet (2,500 m) above dangerous regions took photographs every second. Within minutes of a bomb going off, investigators could look back through the pictures, identify the person who had placed the bomb, and follow them to their hideout.

The RQ-11 Raven drone can be launched by hand. It is light enough to be carried by soldiers in the field.

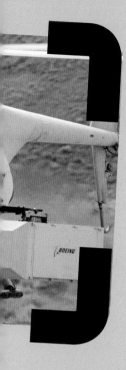

HUNTER-KILLER DRONES

In 2001, the U.S. air force and CIA started to fly drones armed with missiles. These so-called "hunter-killer" drones, equipped with cameras, are remote controlled via satellite by pilots in a control room many thousands of miles away. The United States is open about the fact that it uses hunter-killer drones to assassinate enemy leaders in declared war zones such as Afghanistan and Iraq. However, it is far more secretive about the fact that it uses drones to target suspected terrorists in countries that are not war zones, such as Pakistan, Yemen, and Somalia. Exact figures are difficult to find, but it is believed that hundreds of innocent people have been mistakenly killed by drone strikes, including 18 villagers, five of them children, in Damadola, Pakistan, in 2006. Many people question whether the United States has the right to carry out any execution like this without trial.

DARK SCIENCE SECRETS

The military likes to keep their new spy drones a secret—so secret that very few people actually know what drones such as the latest RQ-180 stealth UAV actually look like. This secret drone is believed to be equipped with electronic countermeasure (ECM) systems, which can make many separate targets appear on the enemy's radar screen or make the real target seem to dart about. Many people believe such drones are responsible for reports of unidentified flying objects (UFOs).

This "UFO" was spotted over Stuttgart, Germany in 2011. The unidentified aircra: may have been a stealth drone.

NOT SO PRIVATE

Not all wars are fought on battlefields. Terrorist groups sometimes target civilians, coordinating their attacks using texts, e-mails, or social media. Some terrorist groups try to recruit new members over the Internet. Computer surveillance experts need to develop new technology to monitor electronic communications so they can help fighting forces and governments prevent attacks.

ALWAYS LISTENING

Militaries and their governments work hard to protect their own secrets, but they are also trying to find ways to discover the secrets of their enemies. Computers are getting very good at going through lots of data, looking through chat rooms, social media, and private websites, and identifying conversations that could be about terrorist threats to the public. In cities such as London or New York City, security cameras watch the streets. Secretly placed microphones listen for gunshots or bomb blasts, and can warn the authorities of possible attacks within seconds. Because of this intelligence gathering, at least 18 terrorist attacks were stopped before they started in 2017. This included a plan by a former U.S. marine to attack a popular tourist spot in San Francisco, and a plan by two men to assassinate British Prime Minister Theresa May.

Surveillance teams use software that alerts them to "dangerous" words in e-mails and texts, such as "gun."

Facial recognition systems study each person's face shape and skin texture, including lines, moles, and pores.

In the image: [TCH]
John Doe
AGE 35   HEIGHT 5'11"
Occupation Manager
Interests Technology, VR, Travel
Location London
57834   HASHCODE 2AB4 CF23 EF98 DA57
M 89342865784357826578S   DB GeneralPublic2A

TOMORROW'S SECRETS

The Internet of Things (IoT) is all the devices that contain tiny computers and are connected to the Internet. Surprisingly, this includes many vehicles; some home appliances, such as kettles and fridges; and traffic lights. Such items are useful because they can be monitored and controlled from a distance. However, militaries are working on technology that would allow them to turn these items into surveillance tools for watching and listening to suspects. Many people worry that most appliances have poor security and can be easily hacked, by criminals as well as militaries. In 2018, for example, Internet-linked CloudPets cuddly toys were removed from sale, after it was noticed how easily hackers could turn their microphones into listening devices.

FACIAL RECOGNITION

Facial recognition technology works by comparing facial features to faces in a database. In the near future, facial recognition software will be able to identify any individual through images spotted on camera, even if that person has tried to disguise themselves. Programs such as the GaussianFace algorithm can recognize individuals at a better rate than most humans. The U.S. and Chinese armies, along with many private companies, are looking at using this technology to track people who might be threats, such as terrorists. With this information, the military could send out drones to target and assassinate individuals, wherever they are in the world. As with all surveillance technologies, this raises questions about what our laws should and should not allow.

CHAPTER 6

WHAT NEXT?

Military technology has always kept pace with new scientific breakthroughs—and spurred on new inventions in the fields of communication, computers, and transportation. New developments reflect the way technology is also changing our daily lives—faster computers, smarter robots, and new forms of transportation.

This apparatus makes two atoms swap energy back and forth. It could be used in computers made in the future.

BREAKING THE SIZE BARRIER

Over the last few decades, computers have become faster. It takes today's supercomputers just minutes to work through the trillions of possible combinations to break encryption codes. To make—and break—harder encryption codes, computers need to get even faster. However, there is a limit to how much faster our computers can work, because there is a limit to how small we can make the already tiny **circuits** through which we move electronic data. The smallest circuits created are just 15 nanometers (1.5 billionths of a meter) wide. However, scientists and engineers are working on new computers that do not use electronic circuits at all and could be many times more powerful than the most powerful computers we use today. Their plans sound like science fiction, but they could soon be real!

REINVENTING COMPUTERS

Our current computers send data as tiny pulses of electricity around circuits, just like electricity in wires turns on light bulbs. At the moment, scientists are working on **quantum computers**. These computers would use atoms and other tiny particles to store and pass on information. Another developing technology is **optical computers**. These computers could use light instead of electricity to send data.

Tiny quantum processors like this one could soon replace the supercomputers used by militaries.

TOMORROW'S SECRETS

One possible future method of computing involves nano-electronics. "Nano" means very tiny. This method could make use of tiny computers implanted into our bodies. These devices could work directly from our brain signals, which travel along our nerves as electrical signals. We could think computer commands rather than typing them. This would have huge implications for military computer technology, including code encryption and decryption. The "key" to any code could be your own thought patterns, which are impossible for anyone else to copy.

WARS IN SPACE

Militaries already make use of space for surveillance and GPS satellites to oversee military operations, such as battles, on Earth, but it is possible that new technology could turn space itself into a battleground.

In the future, military experts believe weapons could be fired from space, allowing countries that have satellite technology to wage war on Earth from stations outside our atmosphere. This would be a very dangerous direction for technology to take and would violate the Outer Space Treaty. This treaty was signed in 1967 by the United States, United Kingdom, and Soviet Union, promising never to use **weapons of mass destruction (WoMD)** in space. More than 107 countries have now signed this treaty to keep space from becoming a battlefield.

SPACE BATTLEFIELDS

One type of space weapon that has been researched by the U.S. military is **kinetic orbital weapons**. Such weapons could be launched by a satellite in orbit around Earth. The weapons would get their destructive force only from their kinetic energy, or speed, as they fell faster and faster to Earth.

Another type of technology that could be put into practice is a force field. This could use a barrier of energy or particles to protect a region from missile attacks. In the future, perhaps a technology such as this could even be used to protect Earth from large space rocks.

Today, military satellites simply watch events on the ground. In the future, could they be allowed to fire **electromagnetic pulses (EMPs)**?

DARK SCIENCE SECRETS

Recently, U.S. President Donald Trump called for the U.S. military to build a "Space Force," a military force that operates in space. It is not clear exactly what this Space Force could do, but many see it as a response to the space activities of the Russians and Chinese, who are developing weapons that could destroy U.S. satellites. In 2007, China launched a missile that tracked and destroyed one of its own satellites. Russia has designed an aircraft-carried laser weapon that could disrupt GPS and other military satellites.

ELECTRONIC WARS

One way to attack the computer networks and systems that help armies fight wars is to target the electricity that powers them. New bombs and other devices being developed send out electromagnetic pulses. These do not harm people, but attack the electrical systems of computers, satellites, and army vehicles. The EMPs burn up wires and circuit boards, which destroys equipment. Targeting satellites with EMPs could also bring down a country's computer networks, making cell phones, television, and GPS systems useless. Some EMP devices could be powerful enough to shut down electricity power stations, plunging cities into darkness.

This image, taken from space, shows some of Earth's brightly lit towns and cities at night. A powerful EMP strike from space could turn out the lights in a few seconds.

ROBOT SOLDIERS

Due to advances in technology, robots could one day take the place of human soldiers. Although that would keep human soldiers out of harm's way, robot soldiers would have to be equipped with complex programs that allowed them to identify a civilian child or a surrendering enemy—and even to judge right from wrong. Could robot soldiers ever be programmed with a sense of compassion, so they could choose to save the life of an enemy?

Boston Dynamics

ROBOT ARMIES

Robots are already at work on battlefields, carrying loads and, when operated by a human controlling the robot from a distance, firing weapons or disabling bombs. At present, no one wants a robot to make the choice to fire a weapon all on its own. This is because **artificial intelligence (AI)** has not yet developed to the point where the computers that control robots can make moral decisions about human lives. But this possibility is not far off.

AI is created by programming. AI programs use mathematical algorithms to let a computer decide between different responses to a question. They also allow computers to "learn" from past events. This is done through algorithms: if choice A produces this result and choice B produces this result, in future choice B will be best!

Robot soldiers would need to be programmed with complex algorithms that allowed them to tell right from wrong.

TOMORROW'S SECRETS

Scientists working for the U.S. military have set up the Hybrid Insect Micro-Electro-Mechanical Systems (HI-MEMS) program. For this project, scientists are placing "micro-mechanical systems" inside insects as they change from **larvae**, or maggot-like babies, to adult form. This system includes a microphone and a gas detector. Scientists hope that if experiments are successful, they will be able to send swarms of hybrid insects into enemy spaces to gather information.

Insects could have tiny computers and cameras planted inside them, making them insect-robot hybrids.

Armies of drones equipped with weapons and cameras would be a terrifying and unbeatable force.

NANOROBOTS

Nanorobots are very small robots—and they are already in production. In the future, military nanorobots could be thinner than a human hair! Swarms of nanorobots could sneak through air vents and spy on enemy defenses. Some nanorobots might even be able to build copies of themselves using the materials around them. They could rapidly multiply to destroy huge amounts of equipment and buildings.

BE A PEACE KEEPER

We have seen how the military has used science and technology to fight wars, but how can we use the same technology for peacekeeping and to save lives when a disaster happens? Rather than a weapon, is there a technology that you can design that could help fighting forces save lives? Imagine you are an engineer and it is your mission to help people in a time of war.

YOUR MISSION

- Write a mission statement saying what you are going to do, and why. How would your invention help keep peace? How could it possibly save lives? For example, could it give soldiers greater protection on the battlefield?

- Research what you would need to invent your new technology. What materials would you use?

- What technology already exists that can help you with your mission?

- What new tools or new technology would you have to develop to make your mission a success?

- New technology such as bomb disposal robots was developed and refined over many years of testing in the field. How would you test your new technology?

- Would you sell your new invention to your country's military, or would you share your knowledge with the world? Explain your decision.

TOP SECRET

How would you keep your new technology a secret? And what dark science might come about as a result of your investigations? Could your technology be used for bad as well as good? Can you think of any ways that you could prevent this from happening?

TARGET 3

TA

These rescuers are carrying a survivor rescued from the rubble of a building after an earthquake. What technology might help rescuers after an earthquake? How would your invention work?

GLOSSARY

Please note: Some **bold-faced** words are defined where they appear in the book.

artificial intelligence (AI) Computer programs able to perform tasks that would normally need human intelligence

atomic bomb A bomb that gets power from energy released by splitting atoms

ballistic missiles Missiles launched by a rocket

circuits A circular path around which electronic signals are carried

classified Information that is kept secret from the public

climate change A change in global weather patterns, largely caused by human activities

codes Systems of letters, numbers, or symbols used to represent others

database Information held in a computer

decoys Objects that draw someone away from where they want to be

digital Relating to computer technology

disinformation False information

drone A pilotless aircraft

electromagnetic pulses (EMPs) Strong bursts of energy created by particles

encryption Changing information using a code to prevent the wrong people from understanding it

flash drive A small device for storing computer data

Global Positioning System (GPS) A system that uses satellites to determine the location of an object on the ground

heat-seeking missiles Missiles that target areas that are hotter than their surroundings, such as humans

infrared goggles Spectacles that turn heat into a display that helps soldiers see in the dark

intelligence agency A government department that gathers military, criminal, or political information

kinetic orbital weapons Devices that drop objects from space

laser A powerful machine that uses beams of light energy

metamaterial A material designed by engineers to have special properties

national security Protecting a country from anybody who would do it harm

North Atlantic Treaty Organization (NATO) A group of North American and European countries that help each other in military terms

nuclear weapons Bombs or missiles that use the energy made by joining or splitting atoms

nuclei The cores of atoms

particles Tiny pieces of matter

propaganda Information that is designed to support a particular point of view

psychological warfare Actions designed to influence a target's emotions, reasoning, or behavior

psychology The study of how the human mind works

radar A system that detects objects by sending out pulses of radio waves and noting how they bounce back

satellites Objects that orbit Earth

sensors Devices that pick up physical properties, such as heat or sound

simulations Computer models

software A computer program

sonic Relating to sound

Soviet Union A country that existed from 1922 to 1991, containing Russia and 14 other Communist republics

stealth Technology that hides objects from radar

surveillance Close watching

technologically Relating to equipment invented through scientific research

three-dimensional (3-D) Having three dimensions—height, width, and length

ultrasonic Sound waves that are too high to be heard by humans

unmanned aerial vehicles (UAVs) Pilotless aircraft

virtual reality (VR) Computer programs that create seemingly real worlds

weapons of mass destruction (WoMD) Weapons that cause many deaths

LEARNING MORE

BOOKS

Harris, Tim. *Superfast Jets: From Fighter Jets to Turbojets* (Feats of Flight). Hungry Tomato, 2018.

Noll, Elizabeth. *Military Robots* (World of Robots). Bellwether Media, 2018.

Shea, Therese. *Spy Planes* (Military Machines). Gareth Stevens Publishing, 2013.

Swanson, Jennifer. *Top Secret Science: Projects You Aren't Supposed to Know About* (Scary Science). Capstone Press, 2014.

WEBSITES

http://academickids.com/encyclopedia/index.php/Stealth_technology
Learn how to make planes disappear and other information about stealth technology.

https://www.cia.gov/kids-page/games/break-the-code
Break the codes created by the CIA!

https://electronics.howstuffworks.com/nanorobot.htm
Find out more about nanorobots.

www.kidsdiscover.com/teacherresources/drones-uavs-rescue
Carry out some more research into the work drones can do.

INDEX

ABOUT THE AUTHOR

James Bow is the author of more than 50 nonfiction books for children, particularly about science and technology. He also loves writing science fiction. He lives with his wife and two daughters.